INSPIRING LIVES

PRINCE FIELDER

Home-Run King

By Aidan Francis

Gareth Stevens Publishing

Please visit our Web site www.garethstevens.com. For a free color catalog of all our high-quality books, call toll free 1-800-542-2595 or fax 1-877-542-2596.

Library of Congress Cataloging-in-Publication Data

Francis, Aidan.
Prince Fielder : home-run king / Aidan Francis.
p. cm. — (Inspiring lives)
Includes index.
ISBN 978-1-4339-3650-0 (pbk.)
ISBN 978-1-4339-3651-7 (6-pack)
ISBN 978-1-4339-3649-4 (library binding)
1. Fielder, Prince, 1984- 2. Baseball players—United States—Biography. 3. African American baseball players—Biography. 4. Baseball players. I. Title.
GV865.F4268F73 2010
796.357092—dc22
[B]

2009038616

Published in 2010 by Gareth Stevens Publishing
111 East 14th Street, Suite 349
New York, NY 10003

Designer: Daniel Hosek
Editor: Therese Shea

Photo credits: Cover (Prince Fielder), title page © Jim McIsaac/Getty Images; cover (background), p. 27 © Jonathan Daniel/Getty Images; p. 5 © Joe Robbins/Getty Images; p. 7 © Tony Tomsic/Wire Image/Getty Images; p. 9 © Michael Zagaris/Getty Images; p. 11 © Jed Jacobsohn/Getty Images; p. 13 © Paul Jasienski/Getty Images; pp. 15, 29 © Dilip Vishwanat/Getty Images; p. 17 © Scott Boehm/Getty Images; p. 19 © Rich Pilling/Getty Images; p. 21 © Darren Hauck/Getty Images; pp. 23, 25 © Mark Cunningham/Getty Images.

Printed in the United States of America

CPSIA compliance information: Batch #CW10GS: For further information contact Gareth Stevens, New York, New York at 1-800-542-2595.

Contents

Prince of the Brewers

Prince Fielder is a major-league baseball player. He plays first base for the Milwaukee Brewers.

M
Brewers
28

All in the Family

Prince was born in California in 1984. His father is Cecil Fielder. Cecil played baseball, too.

Cecil Fielder

Cecil played for the Detroit Tigers. Prince grew up watching Cecil play. His dream was to play, too.

Cecil Fielder

Prince Fielder

The Young Player

Prince played baseball at a young age. In 2002, he was named one of the best high school players.

In 2002, the Milwaukee Brewers chose Prince to be on their team. First, he played on their minor-league team.

Brewers
28

Brewer Beginnings

Prince played thirty-nine games with the Brewers in 2005. On June 15, he got his first major-league hit.

In 2006, Prince began playing first base for the Brewers. He had more home runs than any other rookie.

FIELDER
28

Prince, the All-Star

In 2007, Prince had fifty home runs!

He received the Hank Aaron Award.

He was named an All-Star, too.

Hank Aaron

Prince tries to be a good team player. The Brewers are a better baseball team with Prince.

Brewers
28

Prince works hard to be a better baseball player. In 2009, Prince was named an All-Star for the second time.

Brewers
28

Home-Run Prince

Prince won the 2009 Home Run Derby.

He hit one ball 503 feet (153 m)!

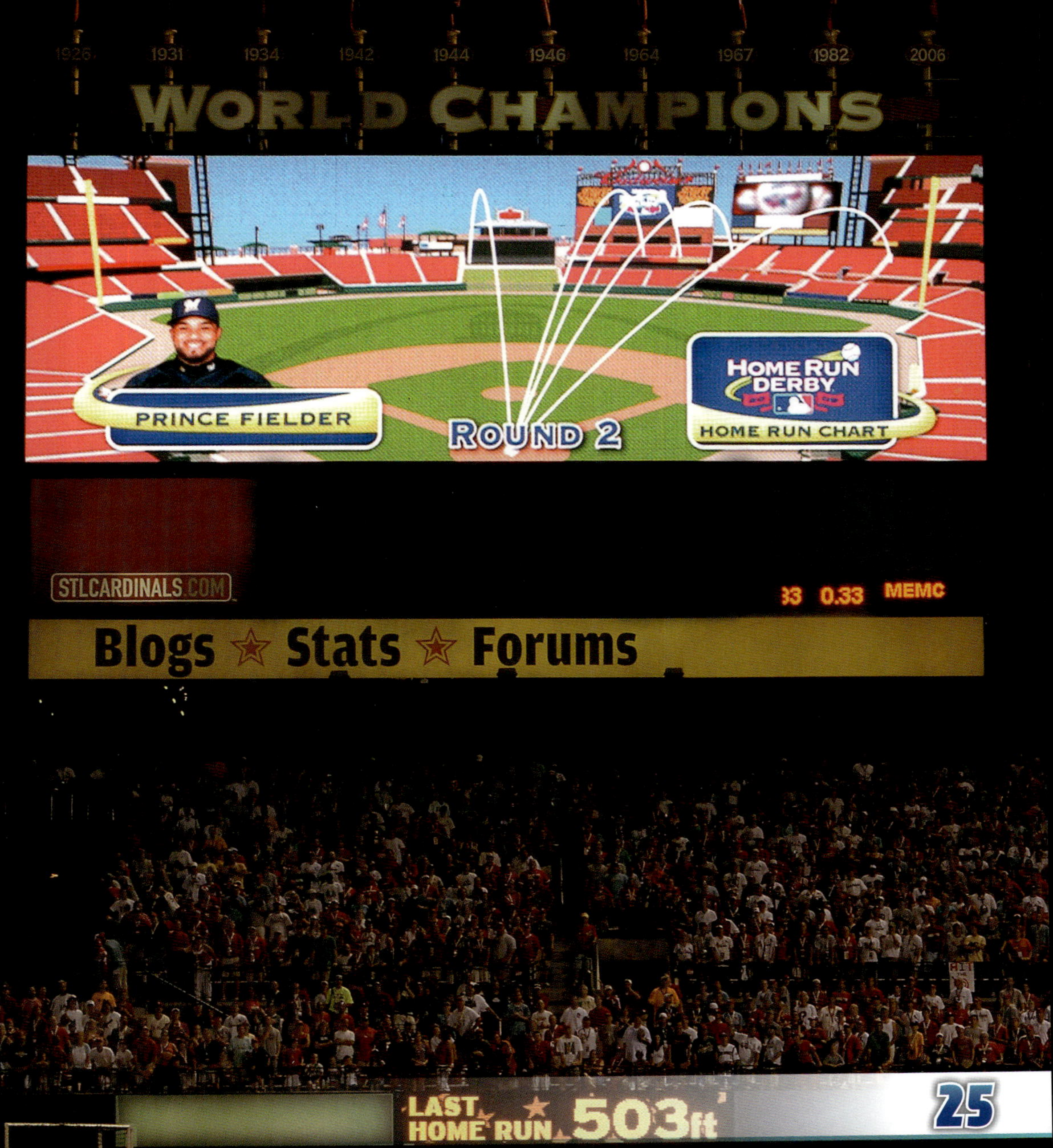
1926 1931 1934 1942 1944 1946 1964 1967 1982 2006
WORLD CHAMPIONS
PRINCE FIELDER
ROUND 2
HOME RUN DERBY
HOME RUN CHART
STLCARDINALS.COM
33 0.33 MEMC
Blogs ★ Stats ★ Forums
LAST HOME RUN 503ft

Prince wants to hit fifty-two home runs in one season. That's more than his father hit. Can he do it?

Prince's fans think he can do anything!

FIELDER
28

Timeline

1984 Prince Fielder is born.

2002 Prince is named one of the best high school baseball players.

2002 Prince is chosen to play for the Milwaukee Brewers.

2005 Prince plays for the Brewers for the first time.

2006 Prince has the most rookie home runs.

2007 Prince wins the Hank Aaron Award.

2009 Prince wins the Home Run Derby.

For More Information

Books:

Golenbock, Peter. *Hank Aaron: Brave in Every Way*. Orlando, FL: Harcourt Books, 2005.

Jacobs, Greg. *The Everything Kids' Baseball Book*. Cincinnati, OH: Adams Media, 2010.

Stewart, Mark. *The Milwaukee Brewers*. Chicago, IL: Norwood House Paper Editions, 2008.

Web Sites:

Baseball-Reference.com: Prince Fielder

www.baseball-reference.com/players/f/fieldpr01.shtml

Milwaukee Brewers: Prince Fielder Stats

www.mlb.com/team/player.jsp?player_id=425902

Publisher's note to educators and parents: Our editors have carefully reviewed these Web sites to ensure that they are suitable for students. Many Web sites change frequently, however, and we cannot guarantee that a site's future contents will continue to meet our high standards of quality and educational value. Be advised that students should be closely supervised whenever they access the Internet.

Glossary

all-star: someone who is one of the best in their sport

award: a prize given to someone for doing something well

derby: a race or contest

major league: a group of baseball teams made up of the best players

minor league: a group of baseball teams for players who are not ready for the major league

rookie: someone who is new to a job or sport

Index